MEDITATIONS
ON
JOY

SISTER
WENDY BECKETT

A DORLING KINDERSLEY BOOK

For Sister Catherine Chapman,
SND, beloved Coz.

Editor *Patricia Wright*

Art editor *Claire Legemah*

Managing editor *Sean Moore*

Picture researcher *Jo Walton*

Production controller *Alison Jones*

First published in Canada in 1995 by
Fenn Publishing Company Ltd.
1090 Lorimar Drive
Nississauge, Ontario
Canada L5S 1R8

ISBN 1-55168-018-1

Colour reproduction by GRB Edtirice s.r.l.
Printed and bound in Hong Kong by Imago.

CONTENTS

THE NATURE OF JOY

JOY IS NOT a constant condition. Most people manage a settled cheerfulness, but this, however admirable, has nothing to do with joy, which flashes suddenly upon our darkness. Like the lightning in El Greco's *View of Toledo*, joy does not merely illuminates our interior landscape, it transforms it. The world becomes different, marvelous and unique.

View of Toledo, 1600, El Greco
47³/₄ x 42³/₄ in (121.5 x 108.5 cm), oil on canvas
Metropolitan Museum of Art, New York

CHOOSING JOY

RUBENS IS CONSUMMATELY the painter of happiness. But this sunlit, unreflecting sense of well-being, precious though it is, is not joy. Joy is something deeper, and in a sense sterner. Although we cannot command it, we choose joy, making a deliberate commitment to happiness (essentially another word for peace). Rubens delights in the positive: the rainbow symbolizing hope (and in itself so beautiful), the light glinting on the rich meadows, the benign cattle and their fruitful surroundings. Yet there are dark elements, too, in the picture, if we want to seek them out:

the sunless woods are not far away. Rubens chooses: he emphasises the good things. Joy is independent of choosing: it overwhelms and suffuses us.

Rainbow Landscape, c.1636, Peter Paul Rubens
53³/₄ x 93 in (136.5 x 236.5 cm), oil on wood panel
Wallace Collection, London

PASSING PLEASURE

PLEASURE, LIKE JOY, comes unbidden (though rarely unsought), but it is of its nature infinitely less than joy. Bonnard's wonderful *The Table* is a depiction of pure pleasure. He has dwelt lovingly on every element, especially the radiance of light, and rejoiced in it. But it is too earthbound to be a picture of joy. It is a snatched moment of sensuous celebration, of food, wine, sunlight, beloved woman; but it is transient, and this sense of the passing adds to the pleasure. Joy, however, lasts, if only in its effects.

The Table, 1925, Pierre Bonnard
40¹/₂ x 29¹/₄ in (103 x 74 cm), oil on canvas
Tate Gallery, London

JOY IN INFANCY

THE VERY SMALL CHILD, who is loved and protected, knowing nothing of the hazards of life, may know unreflecting joy. The anonymous American painter who saw this baby in Pennsylvania has painted a child enclosed and vulnerable, but wholly confident in love. The half-smile, the folded hands, the head resting on the oversized pillow... together these show one of the marks of joy: its absolute belief in what is experienced.

Baby in Red Chair, c.1810-30, Unknown artist
22 x 15 in (56 x 38 cm), oil on canvas
Abby Aldrich Rockefeller Folk Art Center
Colonial Williamsburg Foundation, Williamsburg, Virginia

EMBRACING JOY

WE SURRENDER TO JOY: we have no option. Margaret Neve's girl dances in the moon-light, resting upon the silky air as the great moon rests on the soft waters. She throws her arms out wide as if to float backward, held up by pure joy. This gesture of embrace, opening as widely and welcomingly as is possible, marks the experience. Joy is felt as profoundly "right", as what "ought to be". In grief, part of the pain comes from our feeling that we should not suffer so – that it is fundamentally alien to our being, this even though we all suffer, and frequently. Yet we reject suffering as a basic human truth, while greeting joy as integral to our very substance.

By Moonlight, Margaret Neve, 1994
9 x 11 in (23 x 28 cm), oil on wood panel
Private collection

INSPIRATION

JOY DOES NOT NEED any specific cause or reason. It can come about through the lowliest of objects just as through the noblest. Redon looked upon this seashell, and it is as though he was swept into an insight of the nature of the universe. There on the ocean floor, without light or spectator, the shell is luminous with its own strange beauty. Redon may have seen this only in his imagination, but that is a valid way of seeing: it reveals truth, rather than fact. This weirdly lovely artifice of nature is a proclamation of the universal ubiquity of joy.

The Shell, 1912, Odilon Redon
20¹/₂ x 22³/₄ inches (51 x 58 cm), pastel
Musée d'Orsay, Paris

SALVATION

As well as seeming profoundly right, a revelation of the meaning of life, joy also comes as absolute gift. It cannot be won or deserved. Da Fabriano's St. Nicholas swoops down on the desperate sailors, most of whom have not even seen him yet. The sails have split and the sailors are furiously jettisoning their cargo,

St. Nicolas Saves a Ship From the Storm, 1425, Gentile da Fabriano
12 x 24¹/₂ in (30 x 62 cm), tempera on wood panel
Vatican Museums

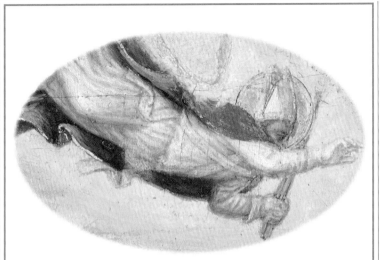

unaware that salvation is miraculously at hand. We are shown the moment before joy, the precise instant when despair and horror will be transformed into the wonder of their rescue. It is unforeseen, a gift. Out of the blue – literally – joy comes exultantly upon them. Joy establishes us so securely in itself, and in the remembrance of its presence, that we can cope with whatever life has to throw at us.

A VISION

THE EXPERIENCE of joy leaves behind it an awareness of our personal freedom. Windows have opened for us onto a vision that we cannot possess at will, but which – having experienced pure joy – we now know exists; and the windows remain open, even if we must, for the present, stay within. Dufy's double windows reveal the richness of the distant world, its gleaming possibilities, its actuality. The space we occupy may be as in the painting, cluttered and even oppressive, but after joy it is no longer imprisoning. We have glimpsed something greater, something of liberating power, and there are no external obstructions to our movement out of limitation and into that freedom.

Interior with Open Window, 1928, Raoul Dufy
26 x 32¹/₄ in (66 x 82 cm), oil on canvas
Galerie Daniel Malingue, Paris

LOST IN TIME

THE WAY INTO blessed freedom may be to live without too great a dependence on the passage of time, on the inexorable approach of tomorrow and mortality. The sense of joy in Renoir's *Children on the Seashore* seems to flow from the timelessness of their experience. It is not a real world, with its softly colored pastel background made up of a blur of bathers and with the children themselves half melted into their context of color. They are responsive only to the immediacy of their sun-filled leisure. We feel that this visit to the beach will be recalled, in the future, as joy, though perhaps not yet fully realized as such.

Children on the Seashore, Guernsey, 1883?, Auguste Renoir
36 x 26 inches (91.5 x 66.5 cm), oil on canvas
Museum of Fine Arts, Boston

RAPTURE

RAPTURE, HOWEVER SHORT LIVED, is a concomitant of joy. It is not a precise equivalent, since ecstasy is as much piercing pain as it is joyfulness, yet joy partakes of rapture in that its touch always draws us forcibly out of the confines of self. (The word means seizure, a strong carrying-away.) Since the face of St. Teresa displays this dual character of ecstasy, an almost unbearable intensity, we might look rather at the face of the angel. His face is lit with the wondering expression of selfless joy. It is not his ecstasy; he is merely the instrument. He is excluded from St. Teresa's divine intimacies, yet he watches her with total delight, lost in the happiness of believing what is not his to possess.

Ecstasy of St. Teresa, 1645-52, Gianlorenzo Bernini
114 in (350 cm), marble
Santa Maria della Vittoria, Rome

WELLSPRING OF JOY

THE GREAT MATISSE had a very hard time as a young artist, and it must have seemed an act of madness to spend his wife's dowry on a small Cézanne painting of three female bathers. Yet Matisse claimed

that in all times of despair he had looked at this tiny talisman and received hope from it. It was a well-spring of joy to him, refreshing and restoring his flagging confidence. *Bathers* is a mysterious work, growing in power the more we contemplate it. Cézanne exorcised his fear of women by painting them: here his women appear gross, unappealing, yet somehow vulnerable. They are exceptionally clumsy figures, held in the picture's center by two diagonal tree trunks, motionless beneath a mellow sun. Cézanne could control the uncontrollable in his art, and that wonderful sense of innocent power is what gives the *Bathers* its immensely satisfying quality. Cézanne was painting his joy, imagined if not experienced, and Matisse drew it from him by a kind of osmosis. It is equally there for us.

Bathers, c.1879-82, Paul Cézanne
21³/₄ x 20¹/₂ in (55 x 52 cm), oil on canvas
Musée du Petit Palais, Paris

TRIUMPHANT JOY

FOR MANY PEOPLE life is a struggle. At its worst, it is a struggle to survive, at its best, a struggle to become totally true. In its essence, joy celebrates triumph. But it is not victorious over others, or over the world; it takes no account of hostility. Joy, in itself, is victorious over defeat; for in that joy-filled moment, and forever after in memory, we have risen above the struggle and entered into victory. Joy assures us that it will most certainly *be* victory, and it allows us to taste of it beforehand. Flanagan's *Drummer*, a wildly exuberant hare, is a comic yet apt emblem of this triumph.

The Drummer, 1989-90
Barry Flanagan
96 in (244 cm), bronze
Yorkshire Sculpture Park,
England

INWARD CONTENT

THIS DELICATE PORCELAIN dancer is unaware of any audience. She dances for her own delight, lost in a dream of inward content. It is this quality of being lost, of sweet oblivion to all else but what happens within her, that makes this a sculptural expression of joy. Nothing can guarantee us joy, or coerce its presence. But for many people, music is an occasion when joy is likely to choose to visit us. Her movements are guided, not only by the conscious will, but by all-absorbing rapture.

Shepherdess, 18th c, Meissen
7 in (18³/₄ cm), porcelain
Private collection

JOYFUL CONFIDENCE

WHEN JOY TOUCHES us it can seem a godlike experience, suddenly making us aware of the eternal, assuring us that we have nothing to fear, and that the foundation of all Being is Love. Like *Diana the Huntress*, we stride out uncluttered through the morning sunlight. We need no covering for our feet: they are met by tender grass and flowers. We need no clothing, since in the world where joy has led us, there is no need for concealment. We may go naked and unashamed, accepted for what we are. Outside of joy, it takes very great trust in another to appear without protection, but here, there is only vigorous and unencumbered movement forward. The dog – our animal nature – springs obediently beside the virgin goddess, our spirit. Diana does not even need to look where she is going: in joy there are no mistakes.

Diana the Huntress, c.1550, School of Fontainebleau
52 x 75 in (132 x 191 cm), oil on canvas
Musée du Louvre, Paris

RADIANT TRUTH

W HATEVER THE TITLE of this painting, Craigie Aitchison makes it clear to us that these are not real grapes in a real bowl. The saturated color, so dazzlingly bright, affirms that this is the artist's world, where grapes hang suspended in perfect

Pink Bowl with Grapes, 1992, Craigie Aitchison
12 x 14 in (30.5 x 35.5 cm), oil on canvas
Thomas Gibson Fine Art Ltd, London

roundness against a clear scarlet background, and where a two-coloured butterfly hovers exquisite in the centre. This is so radiant a picture, so intense in its certainties, that it seems to have, as its real, hidden theme, the absoluteness of joy. There are no half-measures here: it is the all-or-nothing that joy reveals to us. There may be a dull brown lower layer, but it is held firmly in its place, at the bottom, sat upon by brightness. Only when overwhelmed by joy do we know, in our very bodies, that this is truth.

BEYOND EXPERIENCE

IT IS INADEQUATE, even misleading, to speak of "experiencing joy," though it is impossible to find another phrase that can suggest what is meant. Joy is too great to be experienced. It is never our own, never within our power. It is rather that we are taken up into its vastness, and that what we experience is not joy itself but its residue: our reactions, our emotions, after the vision has left us. Monet's *White Clematis* says something of this, if only in its impression of a vision too vast for his encompassing. The blazing whiteness, with the shimmer of purest lemon yellow at the heart, spills out and beyond the artist's canvas. We feel that no canvas, however large, can capture what is seen. In the most literal sense, this is a painting of a vision; we recognize it, not for what it is, but for what it makes us recall.

White Clematis, 1887, Claude Monet
36¹/₄ x 20¹/₂ in (92 x 52 cm), oil on canvas
Musée Marmottan, Paris

REALM OF BLISS

LL ABSTRACT ART is different, and it is pointless to generalize. But there is a certain strain that consistently reappears, where the artist seems to be painting from pure bliss. Hambleton's *Ascent* shows two parts of a richly colored circle, rayed with light, too vast for the canvas. Ruthlessly bisecting these segments is a rectangle, a whiteness flecked with covert and secret forms, half luminous, half obscure. The rectangle rises and then is abruptly curtailed as the canvas finishes. Yet somehow, the ascent continues "out there," in that real world to which joy gives us temporary entrance.

Ascent, 1987, Mary Hambleton
15 x 18 in (38 x 45.5 cm), oil on canvas
Pamela Auchincloss Gallery

JOY AND PRAYER

JOY IS PRAYER EXPERIENCED, or, to put it another way, joy gives us the bliss of actually feeling the reality into which prayer can draw us. We *see* truth in joy, receive it in prayer. Both are valid forms of the same truth. Prayer demands faith and fidelity, and we prove our desire for these by our actions, but we do not need any actions to receive joy. Joy a shortcut to a state of truth, but as in prayer, it is how we apply to our lives what we are shown that matters. Borgognone's saint is now seeing for herself what she believed in all her life. It may be the weaker spirits who, for their faith, need the encouragement of joy; saints can live in the bare reality of joy, without the need actually to feel its wonder.

Studies for the Ascension of a Saint, 1675-79, Borgognone
16¹/₂ x 10³/₄ in (42 x 27.5 cm), chalk on paper
Kunstmuseum, Düsseldorf, Germany

LIFE-AFFIRMING JOY

KLEE DIED RELATIVELY YOUNG, slowly withering away, and his style changed as the inevitability of death became inescapable. *Death and Fire* is one of his last works, in which the German word for death, Tod, forms the skull's features (and is repeated several times in the paining). An apocalyptic sun like a great doomed ball sits low on a horizon, held aloft by Death, like a gruesome trophy. The man who approaches is stripped to his essence: is he humanity moving steadily toward the grave? All this might seem somber, yet the painting is aglow with the most life-affirming color. The death's-head is an intensely luminous form, set in a context of gold, green, purple, and, above, the deep red of fire. With great seriousness, Klee announces that death is a purifier, like fire, and a means to fulfillment. This is the most terrible, seen as the most beautiful. This is the real power of joy, to make us certain that, beneath all grief, the most fundamental of realities is joy itself.

Death and Fire, 1940, Paul Klee
18 x 17¹/₄ in (46 x 44 cm), oil on burlap
Kunstmuseum, Berne, Switzerland

INDEX

PICTURE CREDITS

Every effort has been made to trace the copyright holders and we apologise in advance for any unintentional omissions. We would be pleased to insert the appropriate acknowledgement in any subsequent edition of this publication.